# BOOKWORMS
## MY BODY

# My Lungs

Dana Meachen Rau

Cavendish

Take a deep breath. Fresh air feels good on a summer day.

Air is all around you. It is filled with **oxygen**.

Every part of your body needs oxygen to do its job.

Your body takes in oxygen by breathing. Your body breathes all the time.

Air also has **carbon dioxide**.
Your body makes carbon dioxide.
When you breathe out, your body
is getting rid of carbon dioxide.

Your lungs are like two spongy balloons inside your chest. They fill up with air every time you breathe in, or **inhale**.

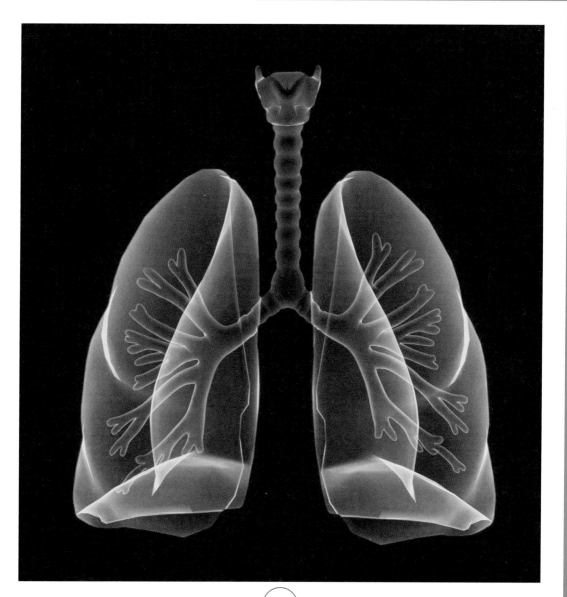

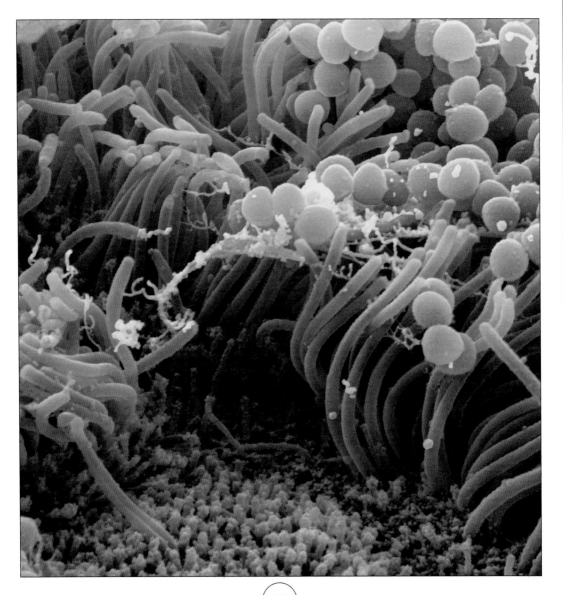

Air gets into your body through your mouth or nose. You have hairs and **mucus** inside your nose. These hairs and mucus trap dust so it will not go into your body.

Next the air travels down a tube called the **trachea**, or windpipe. Your trachea splits into two tubes. Each tube goes to a lung.

Inside your lungs, the tubes keep splitting. They look like branches on an upside-down tree.

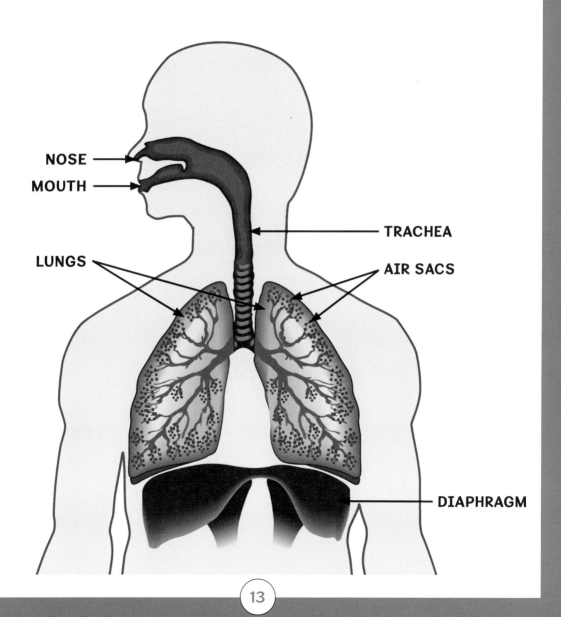

NOSE

MOUTH

TRACHEA

LUNGS

AIR SACS

DIAPHRAGM

There are groups of tiny **air sacs** at the end of each branch. The air sacs fill up with air. They look like bunches of tiny grapes.

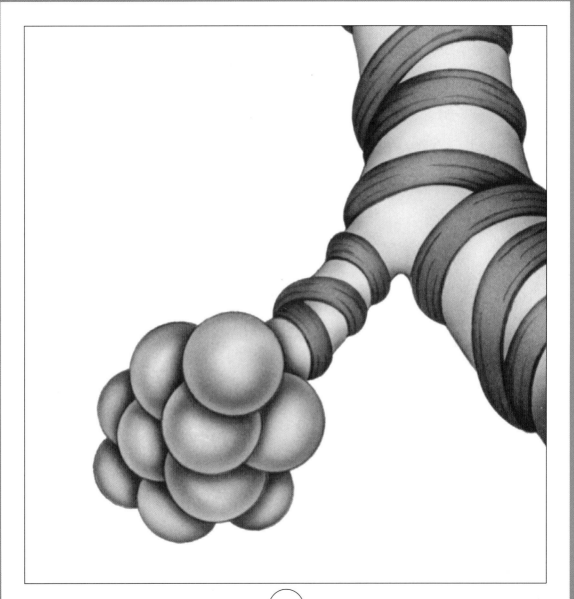

Oxygen moves from the air sacs into your blood. Your blood carries oxygen all around your body.

Carbon dioxide from your blood goes into the air sacs. It travels back up the tubes and out of your mouth or nose when you breathe out, or **exhale**.

Your lungs get very large when you inhale. There is a muscle under your lungs called the **diaphragm**. It becomes flat to make room for the air in your lungs.

The diaphragm moves upward when you exhale. This helps push the air out of your lungs.

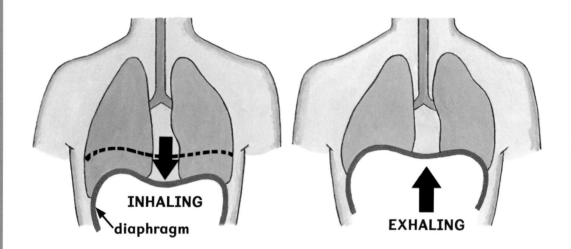

INHALING

diaphragm

EXHALING

Every breath you take makes your body strong. Your lungs work hard to give your body the oxygen it needs to live.

# Challenge Words

**air sacs**  Tiny balloons inside your lungs.

**carbon dioxide** (KAR-buhn die-OK-side)  The part of air your body does not need.

**diaphragm** (DIE-uh-fram)  A muscle under your lungs.

**exhale**  To breathe out.

**inhale**  To breathe in.

**mucus** (MYOO-kuhs)  A sticky material in your nose.

**oxygen** (OK-si-juhn)  The part of air your body needs to work.

**trachea** (TRAY-kee-uh)  The tube from your mouth to your lungs.

# Index

Page numbers in **boldface** are illustrations.

With thanks to Nanci Vargus, Ed. D. and Beth Walker Gambro, reading consultants

Published in 2014 by Cavendish Square Publishing, LLC
303 Park Avenue South, Suite 1247, New York, NY 10010

Copyright © 2014 by Cavendish Square Publishing, LLC

First Edition

Website: cavendishsq.com

This publication represents the opinions and views of the author based on his or her personal experience, knowledge, and research. The information in this book serves as a general guide only. The author and publisher have used their best efforts in preparing this book and disclaim liability rising directly or indirectly from the use and application of this book.

CPSIA Compliance Information: Batch #WS13CSQ

All websites were available and accurate when this book was sent to press.

Library of Congress
Cataloging-in-Publication Data

Rau, Dana Meachen, 1971–
My lungs / Dana Meachen Rau. — 2nd ed.
p. cm. — (Bookworms: my body)
Includes index.
Summary: "Gives young readers an introduction to the importance and function of the lungs in the body"—Provided by publisher.
ISBN 978-1-60870-435-4 (hardcover)
ISBN 978-1-62712-035-7 (paperback)
ISBN 978-1-62712-003-6 (ebook)
1. Respiratory organs—Juvenile literature.
I. Title.
QP121.R35 2013
611'.2—dc23    2012002622

Editor: Christina Gardeski
Art Director: Anahid Hamparian
Series Designer: Virginia Pope

Photo research by Bethany Larson

Cover: *Shutterstock*, ffoto29
Title page: *Corbis*, Norbert Schaefer

The photographs in this book are used by permission and through courtesy of: *Custom Medical Stock Photo*: pp. 15, 19. *Cavendish Square Publishing, LLC*: p. 13. *Corbis*: Norbert Schaefer, pp. 6, 16; Jim Craigmyle, p. 5; LWA-Dann Tardif, p. 20. *Photo Researchers, Inc.*: Alfred Pasieka/Science Photo Library, p. 9; Science Photo Library, p. 10. *Visuals Unlimited*: Pegasus, p. 2.

Printed in the United States of America